WILD
ANIMALS

ANITA GANERI

ILLU...

To Joshua, with love from A.G.

Scholastic Children's Books,
Euston House, 24 Eversholt Street,
London, NW1 1DB, UK

A division of Scholastic Ltd
London ~ New York ~ Toronto ~ Sydney ~ Auckland
Mexico City ~ New Delhi ~ Hong Kong

Editorial Director: Lisa Edwards
Senior Editor: Jill Sawyer
Art Director: Richard Smith

First published in the UK by Scholastic Ltd, 2008

Text copyright © Anita Ganeri, 2008
Illustrations © Mike Phillips, 2008
Colour by Tom Connell
All rights reserved

13 digit ISBN 978 1407 10338 9

Printed and bound by Tien Wah Press Pte. Ltd, Malaysia

2 4 6 8 10 9 7 5 3 1

CONTENTS

INTRODUCTION

You might reckon you're horribly hardy. You might think you're as tough as old boots. But what if you suddenly came face to face with a wild animal? Do you think you'd live to tell the tale or end up on the menu for lunch? If your idea of confronting a big cat is giving your pet moggy a quick stroke, DON'T PANIC! Help is at hand. This horribly useful handbook contains everything you'll need to survive if nature turns nasty – whether you're taking a walk on the wild side or simply popping out to the shops.

So, read on to find out…
• what *not* to do if a bear sticks its tongue out at you

- how to avoid being snapped up (and spat out) by a shark

- what to do if a snake strikes out

- how to keep out of the way of a croc's chops

- what to do to terrify a tiger

And that's not all. This handy book's packed with terribly tasteless stories about people who narrowly escaped from the jaws of death. Not to mention those who didn't make it back in one piece (and those who had pieces missing).

But be warned. In nature, you never know what's lurking around the corner. Or if it's STARVING HUNGRY and about to strike! One thing's for certain. Despite their fearsome features, most animals actually prefer a quiet life. It's true! Most of the time, they're perfectly happy being left alone to get on with their lives in peace. So your chances of actually being gobbled up by a grizzly bear are minuscule. Usually. But mess with these cunning creatures and you'll drive them wild. Wild with anger. And before you can say, 'My favourite food's fish-finger sandwiches. What's yours?', you'll have been chomped into bite-sized chunks. Still keen on meeting a few of them? Oh well, it's been nice knowing you…

WILD ANIMAL ATTACKS

It's a horribly dangerous world out there – and it's about to get worse. Everyone knows you're dicing with death if you pester a polar bear or rattle a snake. But there are plenty of other wild animals that are willing to have a go at you. And they might not be the ones you were expecting to avoid. You'll need to keep your wits about you if you're going to survive. But first check out these six sick stories of some unprepared people who got the shock of their lives...

ANGRY ANIMALS

USA, 2002
Teacher Lacy Reed was merrily messing about on the Suwannee River in Florida when a huge 2-metre-long sturgeon (a sturgeon is a seriously big fish) leapt into her boat and knocked her out. Stunned Lacy later recovered, but she suffered a collapsed lung and five broken ribs. No one knows what made the sturgeon so horribly jumpy.

Finland, 2001
An elderly couple got the shock of their lives when a large elk (if they'd been in North America, it would have been called a moose) smashed its way through their kitchen window and landed on their breakfast table. It broke the table, a stove and a microwave oven before sauntering into the sitting room. I wonder what was on the telly?

Pacific Ocean, 1972
In 1972, the Robertsons from Scotland were sailing across the Pacific. Out of the blue, two colossal killer whales crashed into their boat and smashed it to smithereens. Incredibly, the family lived to tell the tale. Drifting on a tiny life raft, they spent a month living on turtle blood and fish eyes until they were rescued by a passing fisherman.

AT LEAST WE DON'T HAVE TO DO THE WASHING-UP!

Pacific Ocean, 2003

Wild animal expert Mark Ferrari was diving with killer whales in the Pacific. He'd seen them attacking a swordfish and wanted to catch this on film. Suddenly, the swordfish lashed out, stabbing its 2-metre-long sword into Mark's shoulder. The pain was incredible but it could have been worse. The sword just missed one of Mark's main arteries and he narrowly escaped death.

South Africa, 2002

Hippos might look cute and cuddly but they're horribly bad-tempered. And they have massive mouths, lined with gob-smackingly scary teeth. In 2002, a South African man accidentally stumbled into a hippo in the dark. Big mistake. The hippo bit off most of his face, leaving him with no nose and only one eyeball. Astonishingly, the man survived this appalling ordeal.

India, 1999

Elephants can be a jumbo-sized menace. In 1999, a have-a-go herd of 15 elephants raided a village and broke into a store of rice beer. After guzzling the beer down, the boozy beasts went on the rampage. They tore down huts, flattened rice fields and trampled four of the villagers to death.

Why animals attack

So why on Earth do animals go on the attack? Are people truly that tasty? The answer is probably not. Most animals will only eat humans if there's nothing else on the menu. But before you breathe a sign of relief, remember this – there are plenty of other really good reasons why wild animals might sink their teeth into you...

• *Their homes are under threat*
Many animals attack if they think you're invading their territory (that's the place where they live and feed). They don't want *you* in their personal space.

WHAT?

• *They're hungry*
A hungry animal will eat anything, even horrible humans. So if its usual food supply is running low, it'll start sizing you up for a meal.

• *They're protecting their families*
Many animals are especially dangerous if they think you're trying to get too close to their young. Mummy!

• *They're angry or scared*
An animal might get angry if it's injured or under stress (and you can't blame it for that). And teasing or pestering an animal is always a bad idea. A frightened animal can quickly turn nasty and then *you'll* be scared to death.

TOAST? WHAT HAPPENED TO MY KITTY-POPS?

• *They're too tame*
Strange but true. Some people try to treat wild animals like pets and give them food. BIG MISTAKE! Animals that get used to humans are much more likely to turn on them.

A SHORT SHARK, SHOCK

Do the words 'man-eating shark' send shivers down your spine? Then you're probably selachophobic. If not, YOU SHOULD BE! Selachophobic means scared of sharks, and some sharks are the most feared fish in the sea. Take the great white shark for starters. It's a seriously lean, mean killing machine. A quick bite from one of these crafty creatures could easily slice you clean in two. So if you're heading into the water, it pays to know what you're up against. Here are some gruesome great white facts you can chew over next time you fancy a swim or a surf.

SPOTTER'S GUIDE TO SNAPPY SHARKS

GREAT WHITE SHARK

LIVES in cool seas off North America, southern Africa, and southern and western Australia

USUAL DIET: Fish, seals, sea lions, dolphins

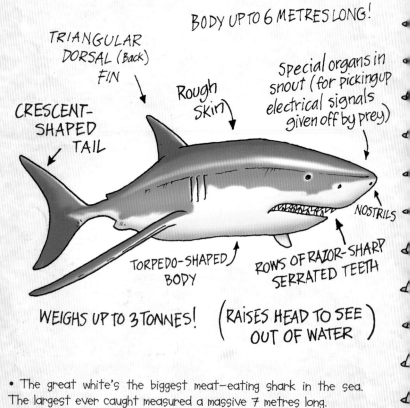

BODY UP TO 6 METRES LONG!

TRIANGULAR DORSAL (Back) FIN

Rough Skin

Special organs in snout (for picking up electrical signals given off by prey)

CRESCENT-SHAPED TAIL

NOSTRILS

TORPEDO-SHAPED BODY

ROWS OF RAZOR-SHARP SERRATED TEETH

WEIGHS UP TO 3 TONNES!

(RAISES HEAD TO SEE OUT OF WATER)

• The great white's the biggest meat-eating shark in the sea. The largest ever caught measured a massive 7 metres long.
• If you're swimming and someone shouts 'White pointer', get out of the water fast. It's another name for a great white shark.

BULL SHARK

LIVES close to shore in tropical seas. Sometimes swims into rivers and lakes
USUAL DIET: Fish (including small sharks), turtles, dolphins, hippos (occasionally)

WEIGHS 200 kg

MASSIVE JAWS

ABOUT 2-3.5 METRES LONG

• Bull sharks like to hunt in shallow water and have attacked people standing in water only knee high. They don't give up easily and will happily chase their victims on to dry land.
• Bull sharks in Lake Nicuaragua were worshipped as gods. Locals offered them dead humans stuffed with gold and emeralds as sacrificial snacks.

TIGER SHARK

LIVES in warm oceans, around the coast and out to sea
USUAL DIET: Fish, turtles, seabirds

FROM 3.5-6 METRES LONG

Weighs
400-700 kg

Flattened head

• Tiger sharks aren't fussy eaters. Apart from fish, turtles and human beings, they'll wolf down almost anything they come across. Unusual things found in a tiger sharks' tum include car tyres, sacks of nails, canned fish, leather coats, wristwatches, car number plates and paint cans. No wonder this gutsy shark's nickname is the 'garbage shark'.

Could you be a shark scientist?
Which of these five fearsome facts about sharks is terrifyingly true?

1. SHARKS ALWAYS HAVE SHARP TEETH? TRUE/FALSE

2. SHARKS HAVE SILKY SMOOTH SKIN? TRUE/FALSE

3. SHARKS CAN SMELL FEAR? TRUE/FALSE

4. SHARKS ARE SHORT SIGHTED? TRUE/FALSE

5. SHARKS TALK WITH THEIR TAILS? TRUE/FALSE

Answers:

1 TRUE. When a shark's teeth get loose or worn out, the shark simply grows some new ones. So they're always razor sharp. The teeth grow in rows inside the shark's mouth, ready to fill any gaps. In its lifetime, a shark can get through a jaw-dropping 20,000 gnashers. They're brilliant for grabbing and slicing through prey, but not much cop when it comes to chewing. If a shark's prey is too large to gulp down one in go, it shakes its head from side to side to hack off handy, bite-sized mouthfuls. Talk about biting off more than it can chew.

2 FALSE. If a shark doesn't sink its teeth into you, you might get a nasty graze from its skin. It's so rough it was once used as sandpaper. Sharks don't have scaly skin like other fish. Instead, their skin's covered in thousands of tiny thorns with backward-pointing hooks. If you stroke a shark from head to tail, its skin might feel silky smooth. But rub it up the wrong way and you're in for a nasty shock.

3 TRUE-ish. Sharks have such a superb sense of smell, some experts think they can sniff out fear in other fish. So it pays to act tough, even if it's time for new underwear. What's totally true is that sharks can smell blood from miles away so they know where to go in for the kill. And when a shark's really hungry, its sense of smell gets even better. Worse luck.

4 FALSE. A shark's beady black eyes are brilliant for seeing with, especially underwater where its prey likes to lurk. To protect their eyes, some sharks have an extra eyelid which shuts just as they're set to snap. (At least you won't have to look into the shark's eyes as it's chomping on you.) It can't see its victim for the last few seconds of the attack.

5 TRUE. Experts reckon sharks talk to one another by slapping their tails against the water. But that's not the end of the tail, sorry, tale. They beat their powerful tails from side to side to push them through the water as they're hunting. And woe betide anything that gets in the way – a shark tail packs a powerful punch.

SCORE:

5 out of 5: Congratulations! Call yourself an ichthyologist (ick-thee-o-lo-gist)! No, seriously, go on. Ichthyologist's the posh name for a shark scientist.

Below 5: Stay away from the water, whatever you do. Otherwise, forget your next birthday. It could be a short, shark shock for you.

Killer shark slays swimmers

Matawan Creek, New Jersey, USA, 12 July 1916

It was a scorching summer's afternoon in the town of Matawan. As the heat became unbearable, local people grabbed their towels and set off for a cooling dip in the creek. They'd heard the warning given by retired sailor Captain Thomas Cottrell, who claimed he had spotted a shark swimming up the creek. But they'd laughed it off. Talk about a fishy tale! A shark in the creek? Impossible. For a start, the creek was 16 km from the sea and the water was way too shallow for sharks. The crackpot captain must be seeing things. Then, suddenly, the shark showed up...

A ten-year-old local lad, Lester Sitwell, was swimming in the creek with his friends when the shark struck. One minute, he was splashing about peacefully. The next, he began screaming and shaking violently, then he vanished beneath the reddening water. At first, no one realized he'd been snapped up by a shark, so have-a-go hero Stanley Fisher leapt in after Lester and started to drag his mangled body towards the shore. Just then, the shark let rip again and tore Fisher's leg off. Astonishingly, Fisher managed to pull himself free, but he'd lost so much blood he died a few hours later in hospital. Later that day, the shark claimed its third victim when it chomped off another boy's leg.

Panic and terror gripped the town and a furious shark-hunting spree began. The creek was shut off with chicken wire. Hundreds of men lined the banks, armed with shotguns, pitchforks and harpoons. The creek was cleared of boats and stick after stick of dynamite was tossed into the water in the hope of blasting the killer shark to bits. The mayor of Matawan offered a $100 reward for the shark. But the shark had already left. Within hours, the frenzy quickly spread up and down the coast. Scores of shark sightings were reported and thousands of innocent sharks were killed. But the culprit had still not been caught. Two days later, a fisherman in New York harbour netted a three-metre long great white shark. Its belly was full of human flesh and bones. Could this be the ruthless killer of Matawan Creek? If so, its reign of terror was over. Trouble is, nobody knew what the shark looked like for sure. And today, experts actually think a bull shark was to blame.

EARTH—SHATTERING FACT

The most famous man-eating shark of all was the star of the film Jaws. And it was a fake. Some real great whites were filmed swimming but they couldn't be allowed to attack the actors, of course. So an 8-metre-long plastic model was made instead. But things didn't start off smoothly. Nicknamed 'Bruce', the fake fish kept breaking down and sank the first time it was dunked in the sea.

THREE SORTS OF SHARK ATTACKS

A) 'HIT AND RUN' ATTACK

The most common sort of attack. It's particularly risky if you're swimming or surfing close to the shore. The shark goes in for the 'hit', and bites or slashes the victim once before swimming away again. Luckily, the injuries from these attacks aren't usually life-threatening.

SMACK!

HMM...TASTES LIKE RUBBER CHICKEN

B) 'BUMP AND BITE' ATTACK

This sort of attack usually happens in deeper water, so divers had better beware. The shark will start off by swimming round you in circles. Then it'll bump into you before it actually sinks its teeth in. The sticky-beak shark isn't hungry, it's just horribly curious. It's only having a nibble to find out what on Earth you are.

C) 'SNEAK' ATTACK

In this sort of attack, the sneaky shark strikes without warning. You won't even see it coming. And by the time you do, it'll be too late – the shark will have had a quick bite and may keep coming back for more … and more. Soon you'll be ripped to shreds and mostly likely dead. Sorry.

TEN WAYS TO AVOID BEING SNAPPED UP BY A SHARK

1 Don't swim* in areas where sharks have been seen.

2 Do take a friend with you. Sharks don't like company. But if you're still caught out, curl up into a ball. Then suddenly shoot your arms and legs out to make a starfish shape. It'll confuse the shark (and take your mind off things).

3 Don't swim too far from the shore. It'll be more difficult to get help.

4 Don't swim at dusk. That's when hungry sharks go on the prowl.

5 Don't go in the water if you've cut yourself. Sharks can smell blood a mile off.

6 Don't wear a shiny watch or jewellery. To a shark, they look like fish scales.

7 Don't lie down on your surfboard. From below, a surfer in a wet suit lying on a surfboard looks just like a seal to a shark. And seals are a shark's favourite food.

8 Don't wear a brightly coloured swimming costume. Especially if it's yellow. Experts call yellow 'yum-yum' yellow because sharks seem to love it.

9 Don't swim where people are fishing. The pungent pong of fishing bait is irresistible to sharks.

10 Don't panic. If you spot a shark, leave the water quickly and quietly. Then ... YOU CAN SCREAM YOUR HEAD OFF!

* These tips apply to surfers too.

SURVIVAL TIP

If you're dead unlucky and a shark attacks you, get ready to fight back. Bash the shark on the snout or jab at its eyes – they're its most sensitive spots. If you're close to shore, shout for help and put your fingertips together like a sharp-shaped fin. That's the international sign for a shark. Mind you don't drown while you're doing this, though!

FIVE SHARK DEFENCES YOU MIGHT NOT WANT TO TRY

Shark-proof armour

A metal suit made from chain mail that you pop on over your wet suit. The suit's made from 400,000 stainless-steel rings that should stop a shark's teeth sinking into your flesh. The suit seems to work well with smaller sharks but a large shark could still do you some serious damage.

Survival rating: 5/10

CAN WE HAVE OUR BALL BACK, PLEASE?

Shark barrier nets

Huge underwater nets spread out around beaches to keep swimmers in and sharks out. Trouble is, sharks do get caught in the nets but so do other rare sea creatures, like turtles, dolphins and whales. But nets have worked well protecting people in places like Australia.

Survival rating: 6/10

Shark-proof cage

A metal cage you sit in. Then you're lowered into the ocean so you can get up close and personal to a shark. The cages are seriously strong but they don't always work. A stubborn shark can easily ram into a cage and smash it apart.

Survival rating: 6/10

Shark-proof shield

A nifty electronic device you can strap to your wet suit. It works by giving out an electrical signal that stops a shark in its tracks. It's been pretty successful so far and new models are being tested to fit into surfboards. But it costs an arm and a leg.

Survival rating: 8/10

Shark-proof screen

A sort of large plastic bag you climb into so you become invisible to a shark. It can't see you or smell you so it should leave you alone. The screen has been used by US Navy divers, but unfortunately it wouldn't be much use to an ordinary swimmer or surfer.

Survival rating: 4/10

SHARK-ATTACK FILES

Havana, Cuba, 1749

The first recorded shark attack happened in 1749 when 14-year-old Brook Watson had his right leg snapped off. He didn't let that hold him back. He later became Mayor of London and was knighted. But he didn't forget his ordeal – his bitten-off leg featured in his new coat of arms.

California, USA, 1891

Some people used to think sharks were harmless. They blamed shark attacks on giant turtles. In 1891, an American millionaire, Hermann Oelrichs, even jumped into the middle of a group of sharks to prove his point. Luckily for Hermann, the sharks had just had lunch.

South Africa, 1942

The worst shark attack ever happened during the Second World War. On 28 November 1942, a steamship called the Nova Scotia was sunk by enemy fire off the coast of South Africa. The 900 men on board were chucked into the shark-infested sea. Only 192 survived. Sharks ate at least half of the rest.

Adelaide, Australia, 1963

In December 1963, a great white shark attacked fisherman Rodney Fox and ripped him to shreds. If his wet suit hadn't held his guts in, he'd have been dead. As it was, it took 462 stitches to sew the bloody bits of his body back together again.

Lady Julia Percy Island, Australia, 1964

To lose one leg in a shark attack is horribly unlucky. To lose the same leg TWICE must be impossible. But that's precisely what happened to photographer Henry Bource. In 1964, he had his right leg bitten off by a shark in Australia. Four years later, he was attacked again and the shark scarpered with his artificial leg!

THESE HUMAN LEGS ARE REPEATING ON ME!

OTHER SINISTER SEA CREATURES

Apart from sharp-toothed sharks, there are plenty of other killer fish in the sea (OK, so strictly speaking some of the creatures on this list aren't actually fish). And they're armed and dangerous.

1. Sea wasp

Feel like you've stuck your arm in a bucket of fire? You've mostly likely been stung by a sea wasp. Only it's not a wasp but a killer jellyfish and its sting is a million times worse. Brush against its deadly, stinging tentacles and you could be dead in less than three minutes. Sea wasps are found off Australian beaches where they kill *five times* as many people as sharks.

Danger rating: * * * * *

SURVIVAL TIP

Swimmers entering sea wasp–infested waters used to wear tights not only on their legs but on their arms and heads as well. OK, so they looked silly but the tights protected them from jellyfish stings. Today, they've swapped their tights for specially designed 'stinger suits' that fit over their wetsuit or swimming cossie. So their safety's a lot 'tighter' now.

①

2. Blue-ringed octopus

Got a tingling feeling around your mouth? That's the first you'll know if a blue-ringed octopus has bitten you. This odious octopus from Australia measures just 10 cm across. But if this little beauty bites you, you're in big trouble. Its spit is so deadly poisonous; it can kill you in 10–20 minutes. By the time the tingling begins, it may already be too late.

Danger rating: ✳ ✳ ✳ ✳

3. Stonefish

Trodden on any sharp rocks recently? Got an excruciating pain in your foot? Then you've probably stomped on a stonefish. A stonefish's lumpy shape and dull colour make it look more like a stone than a fish – until you tread on it, that is. Then it'll spear you with its sinister spines. They're loaded with lethal poison and so sharp they can stab through the soles of your shoes. Horribly painful but not usually life-threatening.

Danger rating: ✳ ✳ ✳

4. Cone shell

Finding it difficult to move, speak or breathe? Made the mistake of picking up a cone shell? Cone shells may be beautiful to look at but never pick one up. You'll get a deadly dose of poison from its dart-like tooth. Within a few minutes, you won't be able to move. A few hours later, you'll be dead. Luckily, injuries from cone shells are rare, but you have been warned.

Danger rating: ✳ ✳ ✳ ✳

5. Stingray

Feel like you've been speared with a sharp spike? Seen any stingrays nearby? Mess with a stingray and you might not live to tell the tale. To fend off an attacker, a stingray whips round and stabs its victim with the long, thin spike on its tail. But you'd be horribly unlucky. Stingrays usually prefer a quiet life, but they'll lash out if they've been hemmed into a corner with no way of escape.

Danger rating: ✳ ✳ ✳

BEAR-LY
A MOUTHFUL

It's one thing snuggling up to a sweet, little teddy when you can't get off to sleep. (Oops, your secret's out of the bag. Sorry.) But get in the way of a real live bear and it might be your last bear hug EVER. A bear might look cute and cuddly but get too close and it could kill you with a single swipe of its big, hairy paw. So how can you be bear aware? Here are the bear facts of survival if you're setting out into bear country.

SPOTTER'S GUIDE TO BEASTLY BEARS

GRIZZLY BEAR (OR BROWN BEAR)

LIVES in the USA, Canada, Russia, Eastern Europe
USUAL DIET: Roots, berries, insect grubs, small rodents, salmon

ABOUT 1.7–2.8 METRES TALL

Hump of muscle over shoulders, gives extra strength to arms

LONG SHAGGY COAT

WEIGHS 500 KG

Powerful body

BROWN, BLACK OR CREAM FUR WITH WHITE TIPS

POWERFUL LEGS FOR CHARGING AT UP TO 50 KM/h

Curved claws up to 15cm long for digging up food

LARGE SNOUT

- They're called grizzly because their fur's dark apart from the white tips, giving them a grizzled appearance – not because they're in a bad mood.
- Bears use their sense of smell to find food and can smell one hundred times better than humans.

BLACK BEAR

LIVES in North American forests
USUAL DIET: Plants, fruit, ants, grubs, honey, nuts, fish, dead animals

ABOUT 1.8 METRES LONG

WEIGHS
70-180 KG

BLACK, BROWN →
OR FAIR FUR

← BROWN
MUZZLE

6 cm-long
claws

- Black bears have only killed 35 people in the past 100 years. That's because bears are much more frightened of people than people are of them. Usually.
- Black bears don't do sharing. So don't even think of getting between a bear and its grub. It could end in a fatal food fight.

POLAR BEAR

LIVES on and around the Arctic Ocean
USUAL DIET: Seals, especially ringed seals

ABOUT 2.5 METRES TALL

SMALL EARS TO
CUT DOWN HEAT
LOSS

WHITE OR CREAM FUR

WEIGHS
300 –
600 KG

BLACK
NOSE →

Thick
fur
coat

Very sharp claws

PARTLY WEBBED FEET FOR SWIMMING

- Polar bears are the biggest meat-eaters on land. And the only bears known to stalk and hunt humans. Deliberately.
- Polar bears are crafty hunters. They sneak up to seals' breathing holes in the ice, then grab the seals when they come up for air.

A grisly tale

Western USA, August–September 1823

Hugh Glass started off as a pirate but gave up his life at sea and became a fur trapper. Then he was hired as a guide on an expedition exploring the American Wild West. It nearly turned into his last-ever job.

In August 1823, Glass set off alone into the forest to find the safest route to take. Rounding a corner, he found himself face to face with a grizzly bear and her two cubs. Before Glass could reach his rifle, the bear attacked. Using only his knife and his bare hands, Glass wrestled the bear to the ground and killed it. But the attack left him badly bitten and mauled. When his companions found him, he was barely breathing. Two men, John Fitzgerald and Jim

34

Bridger, were left behind to bury him when he eventually died. But three days later, Glass was still alive. Fed up with waiting, Fitzgerald and Bridger dug a grave and dumped Glass in it anyway. Then they scarpered, leaving him for dead.

Glass woke up a few days later and you could say his situation was grave. His leg was badly broken and maggots had infested his wounds. But he wasn't finished yet. He put a makeshift splint on his leg and starting crawling to Fort Kiowa … over 300 km away! He had only some wild berries and roots to eat. And the pain got so bad that he kept passing out. But somehow he made it. Half-dead and exhausted, he reached the Cheyenne River, where he made a raft from a tree trunk. Then he floated down the river to the fort, and safety. Incredibly – and against appalling odds – he'd lived to tell the tale.

EARTH—SHATTERING FACT

Black bears in Yosemite National Park, USA, regularly break into cars and wolf down park-goers' picnics. This horrible habit's called car clouting. In a year, the burgling bears can bash their way into more than a thousand cars. They rip off the back door and claw their way into the boot. Park rangers have even caught mother bears teaching their cubs how to clout!

FOUR REASONS WHY BEARS LET RIP

A bear's looking after its cubs

Surprise a mother bear with her cubs and you won't have time to say 'Ah, how cute!' You'll be too busy working out how to get the bear off your back. If a bear thinks you're out to get her cubs, she won't stop to think twice about going for you.

A bear's guarding its food

Some bears are scavengers. They pick over the bodies of dead animals. But get between a bear and its food, and you'll end up as dead meat. Even if you can't see the bear, leave its food well alone. A bear guards its food fiercely and it won't be far away.

A bear's feeling cornered

Bears are basically loners. They're not great in company. So they'll often ignore you ... until you get too close for comfort. Crowding a bear is enough to make it horribly bad-tempered. It might charge just to get you out of its face.

A bear's used to being fed

Rubbish dumps and litter bins make easy pickings for hungry bears. But this brings bears closer to where humans live and that's where the trouble begins. The bears stop being scared of people and lash out if they don't get fed.

BEAR BODY-LANGUAGE QUIZ

It's easy to tell if a bear's really angry or simply sizing you up. But you need to watch the bear carefully for clues. So it is good or bad news?

1 The bear stands up on its back legs.
Good news/Bad news.

2 The bear drops down on all fours.
Good news/Bad news.

3 The bear swings its head from side to side.
Good news/Bad news.

4 The bear looks you in the eye.
Good news/Bad news.

5 The bear barks or woofs.
Good news/Bad news.

WOOF!

6 The bear 'pops' its jaws.
Good news/Bad news.

POP!

Answers:
1 Good news. It's just checking you out. Probably.
2 Bad news. It's getting ready to charge.
3 Good news. It's not really bothered about charging and is looking for a way out.
4 Bad news. It might also put its ears back. It's warning you that you're too close.
5 Bad news: OK, this is your last warning. Ignore it at your peril.
6 Bad news. It's really rattled and you're still in the way.

HORRIBLE HEALTH WARNING

It's best to stay still if a bear charges at you. The bear might be bluffing. With any luck, it'll stop in its tracks and turn away. On the other hand, it might be about to knock your block off. You just never can tell...

BE BEAR AWARE
Tips for avoiding a bear attack

Stick together. Bears are less likely to charge if you're in a group. The larger the group, the safer you are. But stay close together and don't go wandering off.

Leave your dog at home. Woe betide you if your pet pooch picks a fight with a bear. When your dog comes running back to you, the bear will be right behind.

Keep away from berry bushes. And anywhere else where a bear might feed. That means streams full of fish, fruit trees and piles of leaves.

Keep food out of reach. Bears can sniff out a meal a mile off. If you're camping, put your food in bear-proof plastic or metal containers and hang them from a tree well away from your tent.

Look out for clues. Claws marks on trees, tracks or freshly laid piles of poo are all signs a bear's been in the neighbourhood.

Sleep in a tent. But don't keep food or anything smelly like soap and toothpaste inside. A bear won't think twice about ripping your tent open and having a good rummage about.

Wear pyjamas. Don't sleep in the same clothes you cook in. Otherwise, you'll smell like supper to a bear.

Wee in a bottle. Bears love the scent of human wee so if you've got to go, go well away from your camp. At night, wee in a bottle so you don't have to risk going outside.

BEAR-ATTACK FILE

Could you scare a bear?

Experts have tried all sorts of ways of scaring bears off. Some have been less successful than others. Like opening and closing an umbrella fast – yes, it's true – they even tried that! Which of these three bear-scare tactics do you think would work best?

a) Bear bells
b) Bear-proof fences
c) Bear spray

Answers:
a) and **c)**. **a)** Bears don't like surprises so fix some bells to your shoes or rucksack to let the bears know you're coming. If you don't have a bear bell, shout or clap your hands. But don't count on the bear buzzing off. Bear bells aren't very loud or scary.
c) You can buy cans of anti-bear pepper spray, which you spray in a bear's face. It stings like mad if it gets into their eyes. It works but you'll need to practise grabbing the can and firing before you try it out for real on an angry bear.

How to escape from a bear

✓ DO talk to the bear calmly and quietly. It doesn't matter what you say. But don't look the bear straight in the eye.

✗ DON'T try to run to safety. A bear can run as fast as a horse and that's more than fast enough to outrun you.

✗ DON'T climb a tree. Black bears and grizzlies are brilliant climbers, or they'll shake the tree to get you out.

✗ DON'T jump into water. Polar bears and grizzlies swim like, er, fish. And, unlike you, they've lot of thick fur to keep them warm if the water's f-f-f-freezing.

✓ DO play dead if a grizzly grabs you. Curl up into a ball and try to protect your neck and face. If this doesn't put the bear off, fight back. Go for its eyes or its snout.

✗ DON'T play dead if you're picked on by a black bear. It won't work. Go straight to the fighting back stage.

✓ DO stay still for a few minutes after the bear leaves. It may be watching you from a distance, just waiting to come back and have another go.

✗ DON'T be tempted to get out of your car for a quick peek. Keep your windows closed.

HORRIBLE HEALTH WARNING

Bears are wild animals. If you want a pet, stick to a cat. One man who ignored all the warnings was American Timothy Treadwell. He spent 10 years getting up close and personal to grizzly bears in Alaska, USA. Treadwell tried to make friends with the bears and even gave them names. Big mistake. In October 2003, the bears bit back and Treadwell was mauled to death. A very grisly end.

CRUNCH-
TIME FOR CROCS

If you're planning on messing about on a river, this chapter could save your life. It's all about man-eating crocodiles. Now, most kinds of crocs never harm humans, you'll be pleased to know. But a few aren't fussy eaters and will happily crunch you for lunch. And with these crafty creatures, their bite's far worse than their bark. So to help you get back from your trip in one piece, here are a few crucial croc survival facts. What's that? There's something floating in the water? Oh, that's just a big, harmless log...

SPOTTER'S GUIDE TO CRUNCHING CROCS

NILE CROCODILE
LIVES in swamps, lakes and rivers in Africa and Madagascar
USUAL DIET: Fish, reptiles, monkeys, buffalo, zebra

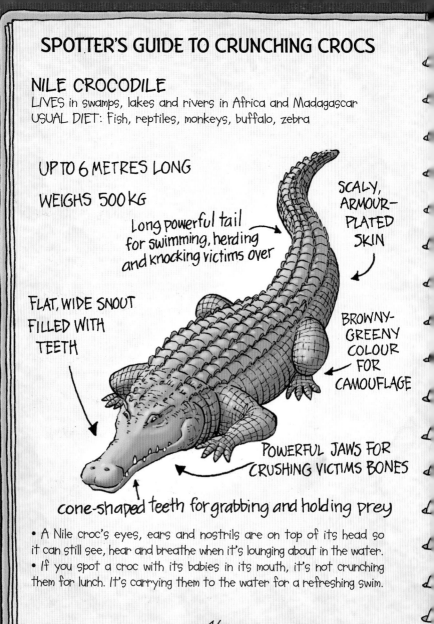

UP TO 6 METRES LONG

WEIGHS 500 KG

Long powerful tail for swimming, herding and knocking victims over

SCALY, ARMOUR-PLATED SKIN

FLAT, WIDE SNOUT FILLED WITH TEETH

BROWNY-GREENY COLOUR FOR CAMOUFLAGE

POWERFUL JAWS FOR CRUSHING VICTIMS BONES

cone-shaped teeth for grabbing and holding prey

- A Nile croc's eyes, ears and nostrils are on top of its head so it can still see, hear and breathe when it's lounging about in the water.
- If you spot a croc with its babies in its mouth, it's not crunching them for lunch. It's carrying them to the water for a refreshing swim.

SALTWATER CROCODILE (OR 'SALTIE')

LIVES in rivers and coasts in South-East Asia, Australia and around the Pacific

USUAL DIET: Crabs, fish, turtles, birds, snakes, buffalo, pigs, monkeys

OVER 5 METRES LONG AND WEIGHS OVER 1.5 TONNES

SALTIES → ARE THE LARGEST LIVING REPTILES

↑ LOWER TEETH STICK OUT WHEN ITS MOUTH'S CLOSED

• Salties like to have their rivers to themselves. You're not even safe in a boat. They'll bump into the boat and bite off its motor. And you might be next.

• Even 1,000 km out to sea, you're not safe from these ruthless reptiles. Some salties have even been found with sharks in their stomachs.

AMERICAN ALLIGATOR

LIVES in swamps, rivers, canals and lakes in the south-east USA

USUAL DIET: Fish, birds, snakes and turtles

UP TO 4.5 METRES LONG   Weighs half a tonne

← BROAD SNOUT

LOWER TEETH DON'T STICK OUT WHEN ITS MOUTH'S CLOSED

• In Florida, gators are turning up in people's gardens and swimming pools. That's because humans are building their homes closer to places where gators hang out.

• It's bad news for pampered pet pooches. One minute you're strolling by the canal. The next, you've been gobbled up by a greedy gator.

DISGUSTING CROC DIGESTION

Have you got the stomach to decide which of these disgusting details are true?

1 You can keep a croc's mouth shut with an elastic band? True/False

2 A croc can't kill anything bigger than a pig? True/False

3 Crocs crush their prey to death? True/False

4 Crocs swallow rocks to help digest their food? True/False

5 Crocs have horribly
bad breath? True/False

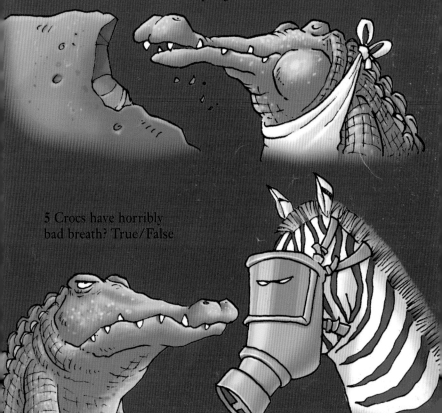

Answers:

1 TRUE. A croc's jaws can snap shut with devastating force. But the muscles that open them up again and are woefully weak so all it takes is an elastic band to keep them shut. How's that for a snap result?

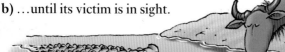

2 FALSE. Crocs have awesome appetites and can get their chops around enormous prey. Take the case of a nippy Nile croc. It grabbed a rhino by the nose as the rhino was drinking at a water hole. For the next hour, the two played a gruesome game of tug-of-war. The rhino lost. The croc dragged it into the water and held it under until it drowned.

3 FALSE. Crocs drown their prey, including humans. Here's how they do it:

a) The croc floats silently in the water by the river bank…

b) …until its victim is in sight.

c) Then, BAM!, it explodes out of the water in one quick burst.

d) It grabs its victim in its jaws and pulls it under to drown.

e) As it dives, it rolls its body over and over to rip off chunks of flesh. This is called a death roll and it doesn't stop until the victim's dead.

4 TRUE. It's thought crocs swallow rock to help them crush up the bones they bolt down, but nobody knows for sure. But rocks aren't the only things you'd find a croc crunching on. Porcupine quills, jewellery, lengths of rope and whole warthogs have been found in crocs' stomachs. Not to mention heaps of human arm and leg bones.

5 TRUE. A sure-fire way of telling if a croc's had a human for tea is to smell its breath (if you dare get that close). The pong's strong enough to make you sick. It's caused by super-strong acids in their stomachs digesting the victim's bones and flesh.

CROC-ATTACK FILES

Ramree Island, Burma, 1945

Night was falling on 19 February 1945. About 1,000 Japanese soldiers were trapped in a mangrove swamp on Ramree Island. By morning, only 20 were left alive. Some had been shot dead; others had drowned. But most had been munched by hungry salties who moved in as darkness fell. It was the worst croc attack ever known.

Boynton Beach, Florida, USA, 2006

Stephen Martinez was diving for golf balls in the lake on Boynton Beach golf course. He was going to sell the balls later. If he got out of the lake alive, that is. As he felt around to pick up a ball, an alligator grabbed his arm. Stephen punched the gator on the nose and it let him go but his hand was ripped to shreds. Even so, a few months later, he was back diving again.

Batang Lupar River, Malaysia, 1999

Fisherman Selim Naruddin was standing on the riverbank, hauling in his catch of shrimps. Suddenly, a croc grabbed his right hand and pulled him in. His friends watched in horror as he struggled for his life. But by the time help arrived, it was too late. Only the victim's shorts and fishing net were found. His body was never recovered.

Vansittart Bay, Australia, 1920

Gunner H. Davies of the Royal Australian Navy was on his way to get married. He whistled as his ship dropped anchor in Vansittart Bay. Boats were lowered over the side and Gunner Davies set off to explore the countryside. By nightfall, he was lost. Then he stumbled across a creek he hoped would lead to the sea. Without thinking, he dived in and began to swim. He'd almost reached the far bank when the croc went for him. A search party later found his bloody body, missing its head, arms and one foot.

Darwin, Australia, 2003

Two teenagers were left clinging to a tree for 22 hours after a huge croc killed their friend. The three boys were quad-biking in the bush and stopped by a river to wash off the mud. Suddenly, one boy lost his footing and was swept downstream ... straight into a saltie's jaws. The other boys climbed the nearest tree where the killer croc circled them until they were winched to safety by helicopter.

HORRIBLE HEALTH WARNING

Crocs are normally quite shy of humans (it's true!) but here are some of the times when you might like to give a croc a wide berth. A croc might just attack you when...

• It's defending its territory – crocs don't like trespassers, so KEEP OUT!

• It's defending its young – crocs are caring parents so woe betide you if you get too close to their nests or eggs.

• It's hungry – crocs might not mean you any harm but they're hunters and you look like prey.

• It gets used to being fed – humans that build their homes near crocs are asking for trouble. A croc might wander into your back garden, eat your pet's food ... then your pet ... then you.

• It's teased or provoked – cross a croc at your peril. It could be the last thing you do.

CROC HUNTER'S TIPS

✗ DON'T feed crocs - ever. It's asking for trouble. They'll lose their fear of humans and become more likely to attack.

✗ DON'T swim or wade in croc-infested waters. That means ponds, lakes and rivers where crocs like to hang out.

✓ DO keep well away from the water's edge. Crocs might look big and cumbersome but they can launch themselves out of the water at high speed.

✗ DON'T swim after dark. That's when crocs like to come to feed. You might not see them lurking but they'll be sizing you up for a meal.

✗ DON'T dangle your arms or legs out of a boat.

✗ DON'T throw old fish bait or fish from a boat or dock. It's a tempting snack to a peckish croc.

✓ DO leave if you hear hissing or crunching sounds in the undergrowth. You don't want to go near a croc while it's tucking into its tea.

HOW TO SURVIVE A CROC ATTACK

1 If a croc comes at you on land, run away in a straight line. It can outrun you for a few metres, then it'll need a lie down. Of course, it could out-swim you all day long.

2 If the croc catches you, try to get on its back. Push down on its neck to force its jaws shut. Covering its eyes will also calm it down.

3 If the croc clamps its jaws around your arm or leg, give it a biff on the nose. It's the croc's only soft spot. It will open its mouth and spit you out.

BIFF!

4

Forget all that if you're in the water and the croc starts to rock 'n' roll. Try to keep its mouth clamped shut so it doesn't shake you up too much.

5

Keep some shellfish handy in case you're attacked. In 2003, a woman in Australia fought off a croc with a bag of mussels she'd collected. Now that's mussel power.

6

If you're bitten, get to a doctor fast. A croc's spit is full of foul germs that might still kill you even if you get over the shock.

SURVIVAL TIP

If you're out and about in croc country, keep your wits about you. Even if you can't see them, there are bound to be crocs around. Watch out for these two tell-tale signs...

• Slide marks on the bank. They're left by a croc's belly as it slithers into the water.

• Piles of sticks and leaves. A croc's been collecting these to make its nest. And you know better than to cross a mother croc. Don't you?

ROGUES GALLERY: THREE FAMOUS KILLER CROCS

Sweetheart (Australia)

From 1978–79, a large male croc called 'Sweetheart' was blamed for biting bits out of boats in Sweet's Lookout Billabong, Australia (yep, *that's* how Sweetheart got his name). He didn't actually kill anybody but he munched several outboard motors and gave the fishermen a terrible fright.

SWEETHEART

Sadly, Sweetheart's story doesn't have a happy ending. This soppily named salty died in 1979 when rangers tried to catch him and move him to a new home away from people.

Gustave (Burundi, Africa)

For decades, this colossal Nile croc terrified locals living along the Ruzizi River in Burundi, Africa. It was claimed he'd eaten over 300 people who he snatched from the river bank. And he was still coming back for more. Scientists who'd been studying the croc for several

GUSTAVE

years tried to catch him in a giant cage. They'd shoved a tasty goat inside, hoping to tickle his taste buds. The plan was to move him to a safe enclosure on the river bank. But the cunning croc gave them the slip and is still on the loose…

Bujang Senang (Malaysia)

In the 1980s and 1990s, a croc named Bujang Senang (it means King of the Crocs in the local languages) crunched dozens of victims along the Lupar River. His distinctive white back made him easy to spot but nobody was able to catch him. Even the witch doctor's magic spells failed

BUJANG SENANG

miserably. Finally, Bujang Senang was hunted down and shot. But his legend lives on. The state soccer team named itself after him and paraded a crocodile skull around the pitch before kick-off.

EARTH—SHATTERING FACT

Villagers in Ijale-Papa, Nigeria, won't have a word said against their local croc. They believe the 40-year-old reptile has magic powers and can cure people of measles, a killer disease. All a sufferer has to do is wash in water from the croc's pond. We don't know how well this works but it beats having a jab.

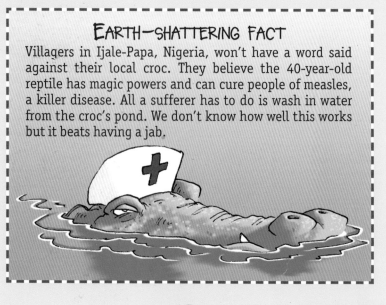

SNACK-TIME FOR SNAKES

If the thought of a s-s-s-snake sidling up to you makes you go weak at the knees, DON'T PANIC! Take a deep breath, stay calm and keep reading this chapter. It's packed full with hints and tips on how *not* to get under a snake's skin. The good news is that most kinds of snakes are harmless, as long as you leave them alone. The bad news is that thousands of people die from snakebites each year, mostly in India and Sri Lanka. So what can you do to avoid being one of them? For starters, here's a spotter's guide to some seriously dangerous snakes. READ THIS BIT CAREFULLY. It could save your life. If you end up being bitten, you'll need to know which snake's to blame so you can get the right anti-venom (that's a medicine for curing snakebites, to you and me).

SPOTTER'S GUIDE TO SLIPPERY SNAKES

EASTERN DIAMONDBACK RATTLESNAKE

LIVES in the south-eastern USA
USUAL DIET: Rats, lizards, birds, small snakes

OLIVE-BROWN SKIN WITH DARK BROWN OR BLACK DIAMONDS

STARING EYES: SNAKES DON'T HAVE EYELIDS SO THEY CAN'T SHUT THEIR EYES

FORKED TONGUE

FANGS UP TO 2.5cm LONG FOR INJECTING POISON

POISON GLANDS IN HEAD FOR MAKING POISON

DOUBLE-JOINTED JAWS FOR SWALLOWING VICTIMS WHOLE!

Rattle at end of tail: For shaking to warn off enemies

1.5–2.4 Metres long

- Rattlesnakes have special heat-sensing pits on either side of their heads to help them track down their prey in the dark.
- Rattlesnakes can control the amount of poison they pump into you. If you're lucky, they'll 'dry bite' you with no poison at all.

KING COBRA

LIVES in India and South-East Asia
USUAL DIET: Other snakes and lizards

FAN-LIKE HOOD

3.5 - 5.5 metres long

BROWN OR GREEN SKIN
WITH BLACK BANDS

Hisses when threatened

• When it's angry or frightened, it spreads out its hood like a fan.
Then it rises up to eye level and strikes at high speed.
• It's one of the world's deadliest snakes. Its poison is strong enough
to kill an elephant in three hours ... and a human in 20 minutes.
• Stay well clear of a cobra's nest. The female guards her eggs
fiercely and won't be very far away.

COMMON KRAIT

LIVES in India, Sri Lanka
USUAL DIET: Rats, mice, lizards and other snakes

90-150 cm long

GREY OR BLUISH-BLACK
SKIN WITH NARROW
WHITE BANDS

• Kraits like to spend the day asleep but head out to hunt at night.
So make sure you shake your sleeping bag out before you hop into bed.
• If you're bitten by a krait, you won't feel any pain. At first.
Within a few hours, it'll be a different story. You'll have terrible
tummy cramps, and fairly soon you won't be able to move.

BLACK MAMBA

LIVES in Africa

USUAL DIET: Small birds, rodents (even a baby black mamba can tackle a rat)

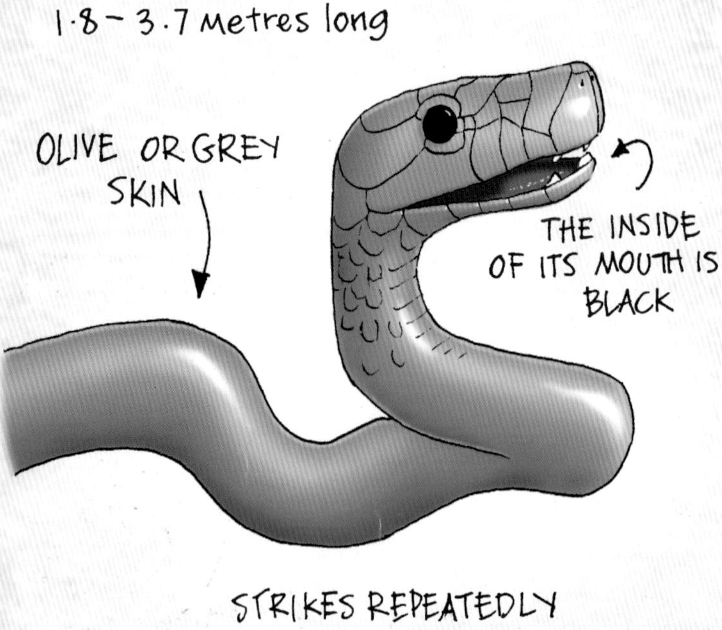

1·8 – 3·7 metres long

OLIVE OR GREY SKIN

THE INSIDE OF ITS MOUTH IS BLACK

STRIKES REPEATEDLY

• It's the deadliest snake in Africa and five times as poisonous as a king cobra. If you're bitten, your fingers and toes will tingle, you'll start dribbling and your tongue will loll out of your mouth. Not a pretty sight.
• At top speed, a black mamba can slither at 20 km/h, making it the fastest-moving snake on land. Luckily for you, it's usually trying to avoid danger, not chasing after prey.

64

TAIPAN

LIVES in Australia, Papua New Guinea
USUAL DIET: Rats and bandicoots

OVER 3 METRES LONG

PALE TO DARK BROWN SKIN

← Dark brown head

LIGHTER IN
SUMMER,
DARKER IN
THE WINTER

• One type of taipan is the most poisonous snake on land. The poison it packs into a single bite's enough to kill 250,000 mice ... or 100 humans. But it's so shy, it rarely bites.
• When it's rattled, it raises its body off the ground and waves its head to and fro. That's when you know it's time to get outta there ... fast.

PUFF ADDER

LIVES in Africa, Middle East
USUAL DIET: Birds, frogs, lizards, rodents

SKIN PATTERN MAKES BRILLIANT CAMOUFLAGE

1.2 – 1.8 METRES LONG

YELLOW, LIGHT BROWN OR
ORANGE WITH DARK BROWN
OR BLACK BARS →

• A puff adder mainly slithers on the ground but it's also good at swimming and climbing. It especially likes to bask in low bushes where its markings make it horribly hard to spot.
• Its fangs are strong enough to pierce through leather so it might still give you a life–threatening nip even if you're wearing a thick pair of boots.

65

HORRIBLE HEALTH WARNING

The most poisonous snake on the planet doesn't live on land. The beaded sea snake lurks lethally in the Pacific Ocean, where it preys on catfish and puffer fish. A single drop of its poison is enough to kill three people so a fish doesn't stand a chance. Luckily, this sinister snake's horribly shy and rarely bites anyone. Its victims are mostly fishermen who get bitten by snakes that get snagged up in their nets.

A snake in the grass
Wyoming, USA, September 1953

Dr Judd Grindell was out hunting elk with his brother, Jack, and a friend. While the other two men went exploring, Judd climbed a shrub-covered hill, and sat down to rest on a rock. He stood up again with a jolt. A rattlesnake had bitten him on the back of the knee. Judd was in the middle of nowhere with no help for miles around. He knew he was in trouble. Big trouble.

As a doctor, Judd knew exactly what to do. Trouble is, he couldn't do it. He hadn't brought a snakebite kit. He didn't even have a knife to cut and drain the wound, or a bandage to wrap around his bitten leg. Finally, his brother came into sight and Judd started signalling to him frantically.

'Snakebite! Snakebite!' he shouted.

But Jack didn't have a knife either. All he could do was hurry off to fetch help.

Meanwhile, Judd's nightmare began. Gradually, his lips, tongue and hands went numb as the poison spread through his body. Soon he was seeing double. He felt horribly weak and woozy, as if his body were floating in the air. He could hear a loud roaring in his ears. His bitten leg had swollen to four times its size. The pain in his belly was unbearable and he was sick, again and again. He was sure he was going to die.

After what seemed like an eternity, Jack returned with a doctor. Judd felt a sharp pain as the doctor stabbed a needle into his leg. Now that he'd been given some anti-venom, he'd be better in no time, surely? But it got worse before it got better. He was sick again, and found it hard to breathe, and the floating turned into spinning. And got faster and faster. Surely he could not survive?

Then suddenly, the roaring stopped and Judd could see again. But was not out of the woods yet. Later, in hospital, he passed out for six hours and woke to hear doctors talking about amputating his bitten leg. He could hear them but he couldn't speak to tell them no. In the end, Judd spent another ten days in hospital, then left (with both of his legs). He was lucky. Lucky to be alive.

Could you be snuggle up to a snake?
Think you've got snakes sussed? Which of these fang-tastic snakes facts are true?

1 How do snakes inject their poison?
a) Through their forked tongues.
b) Through their fangs.

2 Which snake has the longest fangs?
a) Rattlesnake
b) Gaboon viper

3 How do pythons kill their prey?
a) Squeeze it.
b) Spit at it.

4 What's the biggest snack a snake can eat?
a) A human
b) An impala

BURP!

5 How long can a snake go without eating?
a) A week
b) Three years

Answers:

1 b) A snake only uses its forked tongue for smelling so it won't do you any harm. It flicks it in and out of its mouth to pick up smell chemicals in the air. It's the snake's fangs you want to avoid. A snake uses its long, sharp fangs to inject poison into its prey. A snake's poison is a special kind of spit made inside the snake's mouth. Its fangs are hollowed-out teeth.

POISON

POISON COMES THROUGH FANG

2 b) The gaboon viper of Africa has the longest fangs of any snake. They're a gobsmacking 5 cm long – as long as your little fingers. The fangs are usually folded back in the top of the snake's mouth … until it strikes. Then they swing forwards for stabbing. And to keep the fangs in good working order, they're usually replaced every two to three months.

3 a) Never let a snake give you a hug. Some snakes like pythons and boas can't be bothered with poison. They coil

their bodies around their prey and squeeze it instead. You wouldn't be crushed to death. You'd suffocate instead. It's true that one kind of cobra does spit its poison at its prey. It won't hurt you if it lands on your skin but if it spits in your eyes, you could go blind.

4 b) Snakes can't chew their food but they've got fantastically flexible jaws so they can swallow their victims whole. And get this – an African rock python once opened its mouth wide enough to swallow a whole impala (that's a kind of antelope). So swallowing you wouldn't bother it at all.

5 a) & b) Snakes like to digest their food slowly so they don't need to eat every day. A decent meal can last them a week, or even longer. In an experiment, an Okinawu habu, a deadly poisonous pit viper from Asia, went for a staggering three years and three months without food.

SIX SNEAKY SNAKE SHORTS

In 1996, a Chinese hunter called Li tried to shuffle a snake into his hunting bag by prodding it with his gun. Big mistake! The snake coiled itself around the gun, pulled the trigger with its tail ... and shot Li in the bottom! He died on his way to hospital.

In 1986, a South African park-keeper called Austin Stevens spent a record-breaking 107 days and nights in a small cage ... with 36 deadly poisonous snakes! His most nerve-wracking moment was waking up to find seven cobras up his pyjama leg and fast asleep. Amazingly, Austin was only bitten once and raised loads of money for the wildlife park.

Keeping snakes as pets is risky. Dead risky. In February 2002, American Richard Barber was squeezed to death by his 3-metre-long pet python. He'd wrapped it around his neck to show off to his friends. It took four firemen and a police officer to untangle the wound-up snake.

A man working on the railway in Melbourne, Australia in 1989 picked up a snake lying on the track. He thought the snake was dead but he was wrong. Although the snake's head was squashed flat and it showed no signs of life, it still managed to bite him back. He was in agony. He fell into a coma and his life was only saved by a brand-new snakebite cure.

A Malaysian snake-charmer's charmed life came to an end on 2 December 2006. Ali Khan Samsuddin died after being bitten by a king cobra that turned on him during a show. He'd been charming snakes for 30 years and also once spent 21 days living with 6,000 deadly poisonous scorpions.

2005, a South African man let five deadly puff adders loose in a bank after an argument with the bank manager. One bank worker was bitten on the finger and taken to hospital. The man was charged with assault using the snakes as a dangerous weapon.

SNAKE SAFETY – SURVIVAL TIPS

• Watch your step. If you're walking through bushes or shrubs, watch where you're putting your feet. Many snakes are cunningly camouflaged. Use a stick to swish the bushes aside.

• Step on top of a log, rather than over it. There may be a snake hiding on the other side, and many snakes are cunningly camouflaged. Use a stick to turn logs over. The same goes for rocks.

• Wear thick boots and long trousers. They'll protect your legs from some snakes' bites.

• Don't sit down on rocks without looking. A sunny rock's a favourite place for a snake to snooze. Snakes are cold-blooded and need to lie in the sun to warm their bodies up.

• Keep your distance. A snake can easily strike more than half its body length.

• Keep still. If the snake's in striking distance, stay absolutely still. If you make a sudden movement, the snake might be startled and strike. Back away from it very slowly.

> **This way for a safe escape route!**

- Let the snake escape. Never corner a snake. Always make sure it has a way to escape. And never tease or pester a snake. It's far more likely to bite back if it's angry or scared.

- Keep away from snake nests. Some snakes lay their eggs in nests and they'll guard the nests fiercely. Even if you don't mean any harm.

HORRIBLE HEALTH WARNING

There are loads of barmy snake-bite remedies. For starters, you could try carrying a pot of hot porridge on your head or drawing a chalk circle around your house. They are supposed to keep snakes away. Or, if you're bitten, how about tying a peacock feather to your arm or leg. Or you could clean the bite with sour milk, then rub it with a snakestone. (That's a stone the size of a nut that's said to soak up the poison.) By the way, none of these remedies will actually work. But they might take your mind off things.

SOME SENSIBLE SNAKE—BITE ADVICE

What to do if you're bitten

1 Wash the bite with soap and water.

2 Wrap a bandage above the bite to slow down the spread of poison.

3 Keep still and hold the bite site just below heart level.

4 Take off any rings, boots or clothes that will make the swelling worse.

5 Stay calm and move away to avoid being bitten again.

6 Get to a hospital. Doctors treat snake—bites with medicines called anti—venoms. But they'll need to act fast.

HOSPITAL

7 Get a good look at the snake. Identifying what kind of snake bit you will help the doctor decide which anti—venom you need.

What not to do if you're bitten

1 Put ice on the bite. It'll stop blood reaching the wound and make the poison spread more quickly.

2 Tie the bandage too tightly. It'll cut off the blood supply. You should be able to get two fingers underneath it.

3 Make a cut around the wound. It won't let the poison run out and the wound might get badly infected.

4 Try to suck out the poison with your mouth. You could end up with poison in your blood. Besides, the poison will already have spread.

5 Try to catch or kill the snake so you can get a better look. You could get bitten again.

BIG CAT BITES

Has your pet moggy ever given you a nasty scratch with its super-sharp claws or a nasty nip with its super-sharp teeth. Painful, isn't it? So imagine what it would feel like if a cat FIFTY TIMES THE SIZE took a dislike to you! Woe betide you if a tiger, lion or cougar gets its claws into you. Forget balls of wool or bowls of milk. The crafty creatures in this chapter are no pussycats and it'll take more than that to keep them sweet.

FETCH!

SPOTTER'S GUIDE TO BIG CATS

LION
LIVES in Africa, with a few hundred in India
USUAL DIET: Zebras, antelope, buffalo

ROUGH TONGUE FOR LICKING FLESH FROM BONES

STRONG MUSCLES FOR CLAMPING THE JAWS SHUT

Large eyes for seeing in dim Light

MALES HAVE REDDISH-BROWN MANES

SHARP CANINE TEETH FOR BITING THROUGH FLESH

SHORT, POWERFUL JAWS: FOR CATCHING AND TEARING PREY

TAIL 70-150 cm long

MASSIVE PAWS FOR BRINGING DOWN PREY

SHARP CLAWS FOR GRIPPING PREY

WEIGHS UPTO 225Kg

Light, sandy-yellow fur

- Lions have horribly rough tongues for grooming their fur and ... licking the flesh from bones.
- Young lions start hunting when they're three months old but they don't get really good at it until they're about two.

TIGER

LIVES in India, China, Russia, South East Asia
USUAL DIET: Deer, wild boar, buffalo

BODY 140-280 CM LONG

WEIGHS UP TO 280 kg

ORANGE-BROWN FUR WITH THICK, BLACK STRIPES

MASSIVE SHOULDER MUSCLES

Tail 60-110 cm long

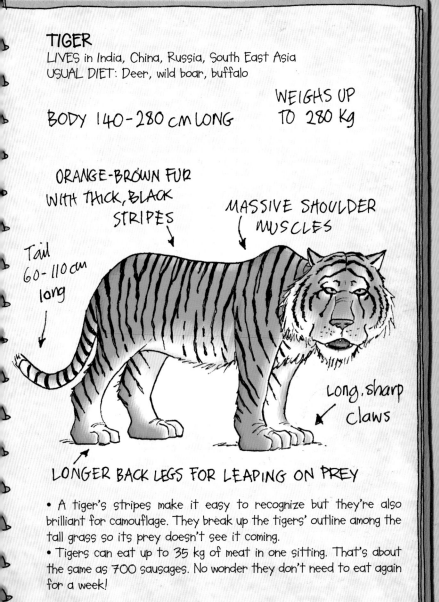

Long, sharp claws

LONGER BACK LEGS FOR LEAPING ON PREY

• A tiger's stripes make it easy to recognize but they're also brilliant for camouflage. They break up the tigers' outline among the tall grass so its prey doesn't see it coming.
• Tigers can eat up to 35 kg of meat in one sitting. That's about the same as 700 sausages. No wonder they don't need to eat again for a week!

LEOPARD

LIVES in Africa and South Asia
USUAL DIET: Antelopes, monkeys, rodents, snakes, birds

LIGHT TAN FUR WITH BLACK SPOTS

BODY 95-170 cm LONG

WEIGHS UP TO 80 kg

SENSITIVE WHISKERS FOR NAVIGATING AT NIGHT →

TAIL 60-100 CM LONG

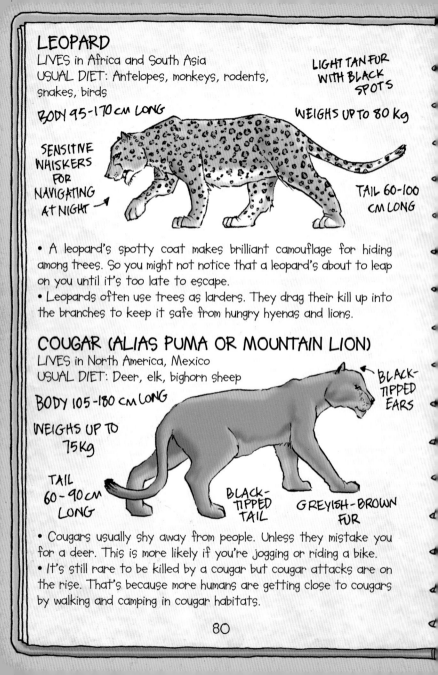

• A leopard's spotty coat makes brilliant camouflage for hiding among trees. So you might not notice that a leopard's about to leap on you until it's too late to escape.
• Leopards often use trees as larders. They drag their kill up into the branches to keep it safe from hungry hyenas and lions.

COUGAR (ALIAS PUMA OR MOUNTAIN LION)

LIVES in North America, Mexico
USUAL DIET: Deer, elk, bighorn sheep

BLACK-TIPPED EARS

BODY 105-180 cm LONG

WEIGHS UP TO 75 kg

TAIL 60-90 cm LONG

BLACK-TIPPED TAIL

GREYISH-BROWN FUR

• Cougars usually shy away from people. Unless they mistake you for a deer. This is more likely if you're jogging or riding a bike.
• It's still rare to be killed by a cougar but cougar attacks are on the rise. That's because more humans are getting close to cougars by walking and camping in cougar habitats.

EARTH-SHATTERING FACT

If you're planning a trip to the Sundarbans between India and Bangladesh, be afraid. Be very afraid. These steamy swamps are home, sweet, home to the largest group of man-eating tigers on Earth. Between 1956 and 1983, these terrible tigers killed more than 1,500 humans. Most of them were local people who'd gone into the forest to fish and collect honey and wood. It seemed nothing could stop the tigers. Then someone had a bright idea. They started wearing a face mask on the back of their head. Tigers like to attack from behind so it fooled them into leaving people alone. It worked brilliantly. Since then, the number of deaths has dropped dramatically.

THERE'S SOME ODD LOOKING PEOPLE ROUND HERE!

The silent killer
Garhwal, India, 1918–26

The huge creature made no sound as it leapt into the hut through a hole in the mud wall. Silently, it padded across the room between the sleeping bodies on the floor. Even when its powerful jaws clamped shut on a woman's throat, nobody stirred. It was not until morning that people realized the bone-chilling truth. The man-eating leopard of Rudraprayag had struck again. By then, of course, its victim was dead. Long dead. The leopard had carried her to a nearby hill, torn off her clothes and begun its foul feast.

It was eight long years since this leopard had begun its killing spree. And three years since it had begun seizing people from inside their homes. In that time, 125 victims had been killed and eaten. But now enough was enough. The government hired a British hunter, Jim Corbett, to kill the leopard. He'd become a hero for killing the terrible man-eating tiger of Champawat. But Corbett would have his hands full. The leopard had already survived being trapped, poisoned and even ambushed by the army. Nothing had worked. Corbett was the petrified villagers' last chance.

Things started off well. A leopard was shot while it was guzzling a cow put down as bait, but Corbett knew it wasn't the leopard he was after. And he was right. Next morning, he heard that another local woman had been killed. Determined not to be beaten, he spent the next three weeks sitting, night after night, in a tree overlooking the river. But the only animal he spotted was a jackal and he gave up. Almost at once, the leopard attacked again. Corbett went back on watch. Over the next few months, the leopard continued to give him the slip. Then, in April 1926, Corbett finally got his prize. The leopard grabbed the goat Corbett tied up as bait and he was able to get a clear shot. Next day, when he found the leopard's body, he knew he'd got the man-eater at last.

BIG CAT ATTACK FILES

Britain, 1703

Thirty-three-year old Hannah Twynnoy is thought to be the first person in Britain to be killed by a tiger. She was working in a pub in Wiltshire when a travelling circus came to town and set up in the pub's garden. Despite dire warnings, Hannah kept nipping out to
tease the tiger, until one day, the tiger bit back. It broke out of its cage and mauled pestering Hannah to death.

Kenya, 1898

Over nine months in 1898, two man-eating lions killed and ate 135 workers who were building a new railway. The unfortunate victims were dragged from their tents at night. The situation got so bad that work on the railway stopped and the workers slept in the trees while the culprits were found. But the lethal lions kept giving them the slip. Finally, three weeks later, the lions were caught chomping on a donkey and killed.

Nepal/India, 1911

The record for eating the most humans is held by a famous female tiger known as the 'Champawat man-eater'. She gobbled down 436 people in just eight years. Local people were so frightened that they locked themselves in their houses and refused to go outside. The tiger was eventually shot by Jim Corbett (again).

India, 1991

When a leopard grabbed Kumari Asha, the little girl thought she was a goner. The leopard was hiding behind the front door and leapt out when she went into her house. It sank its claws into her arm and started dragging her out. Brave Kumari screamed for help and the leopard scarpered. Kumari was lucky to escape. Three leopards had terrorized her village for years and she had nearly ended up as their 30th victim.

South Africa, 1999

Lions that devoured a man in South Africa left so few leftovers that he couldn't be identified. All the police found was his head, one foot (still with its shoe on), a baseball cap and a solar panel. The man was thought to be a burglar who'd pinched the solar panel from a  nearby house. Despite the danger, local residents didn't want the lions shot. They said they made good guard–cats and should be left alone.

Canada, 2001

A cougar killed cross–country skier Frances Frost as she sped past it. It had been hiding behind a tree, then pounced on her back as she went by. It's likely the cougar was horribly hungry and mistook her for a deer. A pack of wolves had been spotted nearby picking off the cougars' usual stock of food.

BIG CAT SURVIVAL TIPS

a) Stand still - whatever you do. The cat's most likely seen you already and if you run, it'll run after you.

b) Stare it in the eyes. Never turn your back on a big cat. Big cats like to attack from behind and it'll think you look like prey.

c) Stand up. If you crouch or bend down, you'll look like a four-legged animal. And a four-legged animal means lunch.

d) Look bigger. Wave your arms and hold your coat open. Jump up and down. It'll make you look more menacing.

e) Fight back. Hit the cat with everything you've got. Whack it on the nose with a stick or chuck a rock at it. Don't play dead or you will be dead.

f) Smile sweetly. Show the cat your teeth. It might think they're dangerous weapons. You hope. If the cat smiles back at you, follow the steps above.

HORRIBLE HEALTH WARNING

Are there any big cats near where you live? Are you sure about that? Each year, hundreds of big cats are spotted in places they don't usually live. Take sleepy Cinderford in Gloucestershire, England. Over the last few years, people claim to have seen a black panther, a leopard and a puma prowling the streets of the town. And they've been munching on people's pet pooches. So are these big cats real or are people seeing things? Experts can't agree. Some think the cats were once kept as exotic pets, then let loose when they got too big. Others think they're probably just ordinary pet moggies and people's eyes are playing tricks on them. (Although that doesn't explain the missing dogs.)

EPILOGUE

Congratulations! You've survived and those scars are healing nicely. You've grappled with gators and sneaked up to snakes, and you've come back in one piece. (OK, so what's a missing finger or two among friends?) But before you start bragging about how brave you've been, let's take a look at how much danger were you actually in. Let's start with supposedly sinister sharks. You see…

FACT: You're ten times more likely to be killed by a falling coconut than snapped up by a shark.

FACT: And thirty times more likely to be struck by lightning.

FACT: Sharks should be much more scared of you. Sharks only kill about 10 people each year. While humans kill 100 MILLION sharks.

So it seems that horrible humans are far more dangerous than any of the wild animals in this book. Here's what humans are doing to them…

It's no wonder the animals are biting back. Being attacked by a wild animal makes a great story. I mean, it's packed full of blood and guts and gore. But the truth is that most of these animals are actually horribly shy and would much prefer to steer clear of you, if *you* leave them alone. So the good news is you'll be perfectly safe if you stick to the rules you've read about in this book. And the bad news? Well, you can take all the precautions you like, but things may still go pear-shaped. Nature can sometimes turn nasty. Very nasty indeed. So, if you still fancy a swim with a great white shark … goodbye and it's been nice knowing you.

INDEX

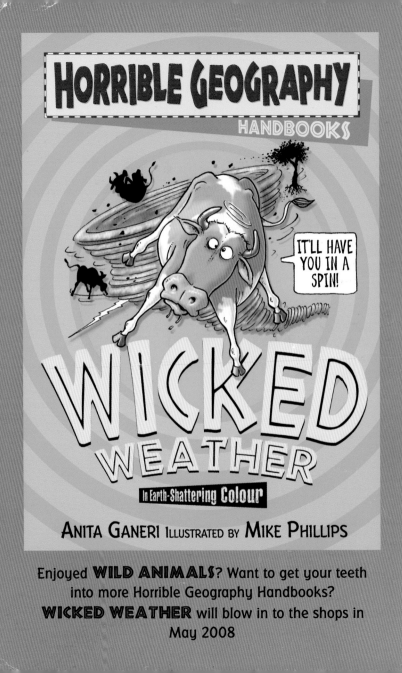

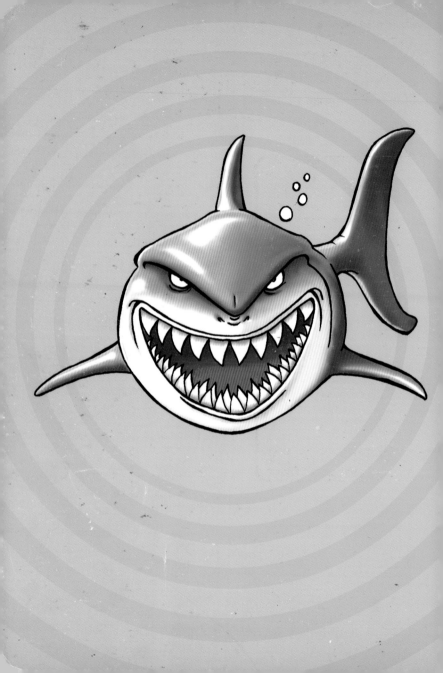